# NEW ZEALAND
# Birds

Front cover: North Island Brown Kiwi
Previous page: South Island Pied Oystercatchers
This page: Stewart Island Brown Kiwi
Opposite Contents page: Harrier
Back cover: Snares Crested Penguin

This paperback edition first published in 1999 by New Holland Publishers (NZ) Ltd
Auckland • Sydney • London • Cape Town

218 Lake Road, Northcote, Auckland, New Zealand

First published by Kowhai Publishing in 1983
Reprinted in 1991

ISBN 1-877246-07-7

Cover design by Chris O'Brien
Book design by Denis Gourley
Produced by Warren Jacobs

3 5 7 9 10 8 6 4 2

Printed by Kyodo Printing Co Pte Ltd, Singapore

# NEW ZEALAND
# Birds

Don Brathwaite • Don Hadden • John Warham

Harrier

# Contents

# Inhabitants of our Coasts

## D. H. Brathwaite

Like so much of New Zealand's scenery, the coastline is very diverse in character. In the far southwest of the South Island are the fiords, rivalling perhaps – though not closely resembling – those of Norway. Here precipitous mountainsides plunge straight into the sea with, in places, beech forest almost down to the high-tide line. At the other end of the country, in Northland, there are long stretches of ocean beach, facing the open sea and backed by extensive sand dunes in which there are occasional brackish lagoons. This region is sub-tropical and in the sheltered inlets are mangroves, especially along the margins of tidal creeks. Between these northern and southern extremes are many other ocean beaches – both sand and shingle; high cliffs and rocky headlands; boulder beaches and, in a few places, reefs exposed at low tides.

Most of these habitats are used in one way or another by birds. Waterfowl and other wetland birds may be seen on coastal lagoons and estuaries. A few species nest inland on river beds and elsewhere but spend the rest of the year on the coast, while a few oceanic species visit the coasts of the main islands to breed, especially on headlands, cliffs and boulder beaches, but are not seen on land outside the breeding season – except for the occasional penguin which comes ashore to moult. Other species nest on the beaches or in estuaries, some in pairs, others in large colonies, feeding on the coasts or in coastal waters.

More and more birdwatchers are concentrating on the group of birds known as waders. These birds are akin to the gulls, being much the same shape though mostly smaller, and differing in plumage and especially in the form of the bill, which varies in shape and length. A few species are resident in New Zealand, but most of them are seasonal migrants, nesting in Siberia or Alaska and spending the northern winter here. A few species arrive each year in flocks, sometimes very large, others in smaller parties and others again at irregular intervals, sometimes years apart. Every few years some keen-eyed observer discovers a bird hitherto unrecorded in this country and so far the list of migrant waders numbers more than forty species.

Some species occur in flocks, others as individuals on tidal harbours and estuaries, moving over the exposed mud or sand at low tide, and probing at various depths and in various ways according to the length and shape of the bill. At high tide, the flocks gather on a secluded beach or shell bank to rest. The absence of such waders from some apparently suitable areas might be related to the absence of a suitable high-tide roost. Other species prefer non-tidal waters such as the margins of coastal lagoons, and a few may be seen on coastal reefs at low tide.

With their variety of techniques the various waders, some, like oystercatchers, quite large and others appearing sparrow-sized, are able to exploit a wide range of prey without too much competition. Worms and molluscs are probed for at various depths, crabs caught on the surface of tidal flats and various small crustaceans and insects picked from the surface of dry sand. A few longer-legged species feed, while wading in shallow water, upon swimming insects.

The real challenge in wader watching is the problem of identification. A large proportion of waders have distinct juvenile and adult summer and winter plumage. The occasional stray bird is likely to be a juvenile on its first migration and if it should happen to be one of the smaller sandpipers, every detail of plumage, size, shape and behaviour must be noted if it is to be identified. Many records cannot be accepted because of the observer's failure to note some small but vital detail.

The increasing use of our coasts for recreation is a potential threat to these interesting and attractive birds. Most of the waders of the tidal flats are competing for an area wanted by man only at high tide. If the waders are to continue to roost here, the area must be free from disturbance. The reclamation of coastal lagoons and salt marshes could threaten others. One can only hope that these birds will continue to find a safe haven in New Zealand where they may rest and feed while recouping their strength for the long flight home to their nesting grounds.

1 Tapeka Point, Bay of Islands

## 1  White-fronted Tern (*Tara*)

The most numerous and widespread of the
New Zealand terns, this species can occur
almost anywhere along the coasts of New
Zealand, and is also found on the Chatham
and Auckland Islands. It is rarely seen inland.
Flocks of White-fronted Tern feed offshore,
where they plunge into the water after small
fish. These flocks have regular roosting and
nesting places, commonly on estuaries or on
small rock stacks offshore.

## 2  Shore Plover

The Shore Plover was formerly found on the
mainland of New Zealand, and possibly on the
Auckland Islands, but is now restricted to
Southeast Island in the Chatham Islands. The
pattern of its plumage is unlike that of any
other small plover, and its nesting habits are
unique in this group of birds. It builds a rather
bulky nest, usually in some sort of burrow or
tunnel, rarely open to the sky.

3

## 1  Black-backed Gull (*Karoro*)

The largest of our three species of gull, this species may be seen everywhere except in the bush. Not everybody realises that the similar-sized brownish birds are the young, and not a separate species. It is a predator as well as a scavenger, but mostly the latter, and large numbers gather at rubbish tips and other sources of offal.

## 3  Caspian Tern (*Taranui*)

The largest of all the terns, the Caspian is found in Europe and Asia, North America, Africa, and Australia, as well as in New Zealand. It may be seen anywhere around the coasts of the North and South Islands, including in estuaries and coastal lagoons, and sometimes occurs on inland lakes. The black cap is lost after the nesting season but grows back by about July.

## 2  Wandering Tattler

Two species of tattler occur in New Zealand, and, in winter plumage, are very difficult to distinguish in the field. The Wandering Tattler nests in Alaska and on the eastern tip of Siberia, where its range overlaps that of the Grey-tailed Tattler. The plain, grey upper plumage, rather long, straight bill and yellowish legs help to differentiate these two species from other waders.

13

### 1  New Zealand Dotterel (*Tuturiwhatu*)

Also known as the Red-breasted Dotterel, this bird is known to breed only in the north of the North Island, on the coast of Southland and on Stewart Island. It is found on ocean beaches, and on the sandy tidal flats of harbours and estuaries. A few pairs are usually to be seen along Farewell Spit, but have not been found breeding, and occasional vagrants occur on the coasts north of Cook Strait.

### 2  Little Whimbrel

Amongst the rarer migratory waders to visit New Zealand is the Little Whimbrel, a bird similar in size to the Golden Plover. It is probably best distinguished by its general upright stance, small down-curved bill and the darker primaries visible in flight. Little Whimbrels breed in central and north-eastern Siberia and the bulk of the population winters in Australia.

### 1  Bar-tailed Godwit (*Kuaka*)

This species is the most numerous of the migrants which nest in the Northern Hemisphere and huge flocks spend the northern winter in New Zealand. It feeds on exposed tidal flats of harbours and estuaries, provided it can find an undisturbed area where it can roost at high tide. Two other species, the Black-tailed Godwit from Asia and the Hudsonian from Arctic America also occur occasionally, and are usually seen in company with the species illustrated.

### 2  Terek Sandpiper

The first Terek Sandpipers were recorded in New Zealand only 30 years ago, but they are now observed most years on suitable mudflats. While some of our migratory waders are difficult to identify in eclipse plumage, the distinctly upturned bill of this sandpiper plus the white trailing edge of the wings, visible in flight, make it an easy bird to identify.

### 3  Bar-tailed Godwit and Knot

Both these species feed on tidal flats, the godwits probing deeply, and the knots just below the surface, thus sharing the available food. At high tide they will form mixed flocks to roost on such spots as the shell bank in the photograph. These are the two most numerous migrant waders in New Zealand, both numbering tens of thousands.

## 2  Variable Oystercatcher (*Torea*)

Variable Oystercatchers, as their name suggests, may be found ranging from an all-dark form to black-and-white birds superficially similar to South Island Pied Oystercatchers. This dark bird was photographed with its newly hatched chicks on a remote sandspit near Hicks Bay, East Cape. Conspicuous but wary birds, they are increasingly at the mercy of 'beach buggies' whose drivers destroy unseen nests, unaware of and sadly often uncaring about the damage they cause.

## 3  Curlew Sandpiper

In 1902 the famous Canterbury naturalist Edgar Stead first discovered this species in New Zealand at Lake Ellesmere. Today it is seen frequently. In its winter garb it is a drab brownish-grey, but prior to its departure for its breeding grounds in Arctic Asia it assumes a rich rufous breeding plumage which makes it easily identifiable amongst our other Arctic visitors.

## 1  Red-billed Gull (*Tarapunga*)

Of the two very similar small gulls of New Zealand, this is the most widely distributed and most numerous. The names of the Red-billed and Black-billed Gulls can be somewhat misleading, applying only to adult birds. The bill of second-year Black-billed Gulls can be quite bright red, and that of young Red-billed Gulls is dark brown. In the Black-billed Gull there is much less black on the wing tips and the bill is more slender and a little longer.

# Birds of the Forest

## D. H. Brathwaite

For millions of years, prior to the arrival of man, New Zealand was predominantly forest-clad. Doubtlessly, during long periods of either intensely cold or very dry climatic conditions, the forest retreated temporarily but, as conditions improved, covered the landscape again. When the ancestors of the Maori arrived in New Zealand, almost the whole country – from the alpine scrub to the coast – was covered with forest, which was inhabited by a small but remarkably diverse bird fauna.

Taking the place of the usual herbivorous animals were twelve or more species of large flightless birds which browsed on the foliage of the trees and shrubs, grazed on the herbage in clearings, or rooted for such things as fern roots. All of these, except a rail – the takahe – are now extinct. There was also a large and powerful eagle, a hawk of intermediate size, a falcon, two owls and an owlet-nightjar; only the falcon and the smaller owl remain, though the larger owl too might still survive.

On the other hand, there was only one large parrot and two or perhaps three, small parakeets; a single very large pigeon but none of the small doves found in Australia and the islands of the southwest Pacific. Of the songbirds, usually the most numerous species on large islands and continents, there were only 22 species. This is very few, considering that New Zealand has a wide variety of quite diverse forest, including beech, podocarp, tawa and kauri, and various scrub types, such as alpine, manuka, etc. There is more than one type of both beech and podocarp forest, depending on the dominant species. In such conditions, a great variety of fruit-, nectar- and insect-eating songbird species might reasonably have been expected.

With few exceptions, the New Zealand bush birds are endemic; that is, they are peculiar to New Zealand to a greater or lesser degree. The fantail, for instance, also occurs throughout Australia, in Papua-New Guinea, and elsewhere in the southwest Pacific, but the New Zealand birds form three distinct geographic races, in the North, South and Chatham Islands respectively. The Grey Warbler, the Tit and the Robin, and the Bellbird are distinct species, but with obvious close relatives in Australia. The Tui and the Stitchbird, on the other hand, belong to the widespread Australasian family of honeyeaters, but show no apparently close relationship to any other species. The Silvereye, of course, having only invaded and settled in New Zealand about 150 years ago, is clearly identical to the Tasmanian species. The relationships of the remainder of the songbirds, the parrots and the pigeon have still to be determined.

The bush birds of New Zealand have varied markedly in their ability to survive in man-made or greatly modified environments. The Silvereye, the Fantail and the Grey Warbler commonly occur in suburban parks and garden shrubberies, and the Bellbird will visit flowering trees in suburban gardens and parks in some cities. The Bellbird, Tit and Robin, the Whitehead and Brown Creeper thrive in exotic pine forests. With the exception of the latter two species, all these are relatively recent colonists whose closest Australian relatives are birds of the open woodland rather than dense forest. Of the more ancient species, only the Whitehead, Brown Creeper, Rifleman, Pigeon, Weka and Kiwi have shown any ability to survive in anything but native forest. The Brown Kiwi still occurs in hilly farm country in parts of the North Island where there are patches of dense scrub. The Weka can also survive in the same type of habitat, and in Gisborne even comes into suburban gardens. The Pigeon will visit suburban parks and certain types of plantation, to feed and occasionally even to nest, but would starve in exotic pine forests.

The continued clearing of native forest and scrub does not augur well for the continued survival of these ancient species, but surprisingly little concern seems to be felt, compared with the indignation over the loss of works of art. After all, the latter can be copied, which is some consolation, but a species can never be reproduced. Extinction is forever.

## 1 Brown Kiwi (*Tokoeka*)

Of the three species of kiwi, the Large Spotted is restricted to the South Island, as is the Little Spotted, which is now apparently close to extinction; it was formerly also found in the North Island. The Brown Kiwi has three races, one each in the North, South and Stewart Islands, of which the latter form is illustrated.

### 3  Brown Kiwi
Normally nocturnal in habit the male can be identified by its shrill *ki-wi*, while the female has a remarkably hoarse cry. They lay one or two large eggs incubated by the male in 75–80 days. The bird illustrated is the North Island subspecies.

### 2  Great Spotted Kiwi (*Roa*)
Still fairly common in forests of west Nelson and Westland south to about Okarito, south of which it is not known, for certain, to occur. It is also found in forests at higher altitudes on the east side of the divide in the Lewis Pass and Arthur's Pass areas. Its nesting habits are not well known but probably differ little from those of other kiwis.

2

## 2 Tui

The largest of our honeyeaters, the Tui is here depicted in a flowering kowhai, a popular source of nectar. Tuis will visit gardens and parks in settled areas where there are suitable sources of nectar, but are very rare in exotic forests. They do not favour beech forest and it is quite possible that the continued removal of podocarp hardwood forest could result in this species, still quite common, being placed on the endangered list.

## 1 Long-tailed Cuckoo (*Koekoea*)

Found throughout New Zealand, mainly in native forests, it lays its eggs in the nests of Whiteheads, Brown Creepers and – less often – of Robin, Tit, Yellowhead and Silvereye. It arrives each year in September or October and departs in February to spend the winter on islands of the southwest Pacific. The bird illustrated is a juvenile, adults having a longer tail and lacking the white spots on the back.

### 1 Antipodes Island Parakeet

The largest of the native parakeets, this bird is seen by only a privileged few, being found only on lonely Antipodes Island, where it inhabits tussock grassland and low scrub. It lacks the colourful red or yellow crown of the other species. A race of the Red-crowned Parakeet is also found on the island.

### 2 Yellow-crowned Parakeet (*Kakariki*)

Smaller than the Red-crowned Parakeet and not found outside the New Zealand region, this species is still common in the more extensive tracts of native forest on the North, South and Stewart Islands, and surrounding islands and on the Chatham Islands. There is some evidence on the smaller islands that this species feeds less on the ground than the larger bird. This would no doubt make it less vulnerable to introduced predators.

### 3 Red-crowned Parakeet (*Kakariki*)

This handsome parakeet was formerly found throughout the main islands of New Zealand and on the Kermadec, Chatham and Auckland Islands, Antipodes and Macquarie Islands, Lord Howe, Norfolk Islands and New Caledonia. It is now extinct on Macquarie and Lord Howe Islands. On the North and South Islands it is now rather restricted in distribution but is still numerous on the coastal and outlying islands.

27

## 1 Brown Creeper (*Pipipi*)

Closely related to the Yellowhead and Whitehead, its habits are similar, feeding in noisy flocks and building a similar nest. The nest is usually well concealed in a dense shrub or, as illustrated, in a lawyer vine. Brown Creepers occur mostly in native forest and scrub but also in exotic forest.

## 2 New Zealand Snipe

Snipe are usually marsh birds but the New Zealand species is a bush bird. Formerly distributed on both North and South Islands, these populations were no doubt exterminated by the Polynesian rat, and the species now survives only on islands off Stewart Island, the Snares, Antipodes Island and the Auckland Islands, with another species on the Chatham Islands. The bird illustrated belongs to the Snares race.

Previous page **Grey Warbler** (*Riroriro*)
Here shown flying up to the nest entrance, it is more often heard than seen. From the native forests and scrub, from city parks and suburban gardens, its song can be heard as a rising and falling trill, seeming weak, but audible from a surprising distance. It feeds chiefly on spiders and small insects and is the most common host of the Shining Cuckoo.

## 1 Rock Wren

A member of one of New Zealand's most peculiar families of birds, the Rock Wren is not a true bush bird but is found in alpine and sub-alpine habitats in the western half of the South Island. It frequents rocky crevices and rockfalls where it feeds both above and below ground, chiefly on insects and spiders. It can survive below ground level even when snow covers its habitat.

## 2 Rifleman (*Titipounamu*)

A male at the nest hole. This species is widely distributed in the South Island, in the North Island south of Te Aroha and on Great and Little Barrier Islands, in native forest and some types of exotic forest. It feeds on insects found in bark crevices and foliage. It is one of the only two or three surviving species of New Zealand wren, one of our unique bird families.

### 3 North Island Saddleback

The wholly brown juvenile plumage of the
South Island Saddleback is not found in the
North Island race, which also differs in
having a distinct, narrow pale margin on the
front edge of the brown "saddle". Not so
many years ago this race survived only on
Chicken Island, but transfers of birds to
other suitable islands have resulted in a
dramatic increase in numbers and a greater
chance of its survival.

### 4 Stead's Bush Wren (*Matuhi*)

If the Bush Wren still exists on the North or
South Islands it is certainly very rare. The
race formerly found on the islands around
Stewart Island was exterminated by rats so
that the species, if not wholly extinct, must
be regarded as endangered. It is difficult to
understand why the Bush Wren should have
disappeared when the Rifleman is still
widespread.

### 1 Morepork (*Ruru*)

The smaller of our two native owls, this is still a common bird though less so in some districts than in others. Other races of this species are found on Norfolk and Lord Howe Islands, throughout Australia – where it has the name "Boobook" – to the Lesser Sunda Islands and southern New Guinea. It feeds chiefly on insects, as in the illustration, but also on small birds, rats, mice and lizards. There have been no accepted records of sightings of the other New Zealand species, the Laughing Owl, since 1914.

### 2 New Zealand Falcon (*Karearea*)

Also known as the Bush Hawk, this bold and fierce hunter is still not uncommon in the hilly back country. Its normal prey consists mainly of birds, including various introduced species, but small mammals are also taken. It is particularly fearless in defence of its breeding territory and will attack even humans who may unknowingly trespass. The female is normally distinctly larger and more intensely coloured than the male.

## 1 Kakapo

It seems that, as recently as 50 years ago, the Kakapo was still not uncommon in the South Island mountain forests, though extinct in the North Island. The wings are large enough to permit the bird to glide downward but it cannot take off and progresses mainly on foot. In the courting season, the males scrape out dust bowls from which they "boom" competitively to attract the females. The bird illustrated is a male engaged in "booming".

## 2 Kea

Nesting in the bush not too far below the tree line, the Kea is better known as a bird of subalpine regions and high country pasture, where it has a bad reputation for killing sheep. Very few people seem to have witnessed this behaviour but there is little doubt that at least some birds are guilty. The bird is highly intelligent and mischievous in other ways also and trampers and campers quickly learn the destructive power of its fearsome-looking bill.

## 3 Kaka

This parrot is a bird of the larger tracts of native forest on the North, South and Stewart Island, and on such coastal islands as Great and Little Barrier and Kapiti. Its numbers have decreased greatly during the past hundred years. North Island birds are smaller and rather duller in colouring; the bird illustrated belongs to the South Island race. Its food is mainly fruit and insects, especially the larvae of wood-boring insects, and it also eats leaves and nectar.

## 1 Kokako

With the Saddleback and the extinct Huia, the Kokako belongs to the ancient family of New Zealand wattlebirds and is the only species of the three still surviving on the mainland. North Island birds, shown here with young at the nest, have bright blue wattles in the adult, flesh-coloured in the young birds. The South Island Kokako, possibly extinct, has orange wattles. It feeds on leaves, flowers and fruit of native trees.

## 2 Pigeon (*Kereru*)

The only species of pigeon indigenous to New Zealand, this bird has no known relatives outside this country apart from a race, now extinct, in Norfolk Island. It is shown here on a kowhai tree of which the flowers, together with those of some introduced trees such as broom, are an important food. It also eats the leaves and fruit of a large number of other native trees and certain introduced trees, and will also eat clover.

## 1 Takahe

The rails are a family of birds many of which have become flightless in New Zealand. The Takahe is obviously descended from a species like the Pukeko but, like the Weka, has forsaken the wetland for a woodland habitat. In its last refuge, in Fiordland, the species inhabits snowgrass tussock grassland in summer and retreats into the bush when the snow of winter arrives. Before its dramatic rediscovery by Dr Orbell, it was believed to be extinct.

## 2 Weka

The weka seems to bear much the same relationship to the Banded Rail as the Takahe does to the Pukeko. Apparently descended from a common ancestor that arrived in an earlier invasion, it has become more of a bush bird than one of the wetlands, and in the absence of ground predators has lost the power of flight. The name "Weka" is no doubt cognate with "Veka" and similar names used in Polynesia for the Banded Rail.

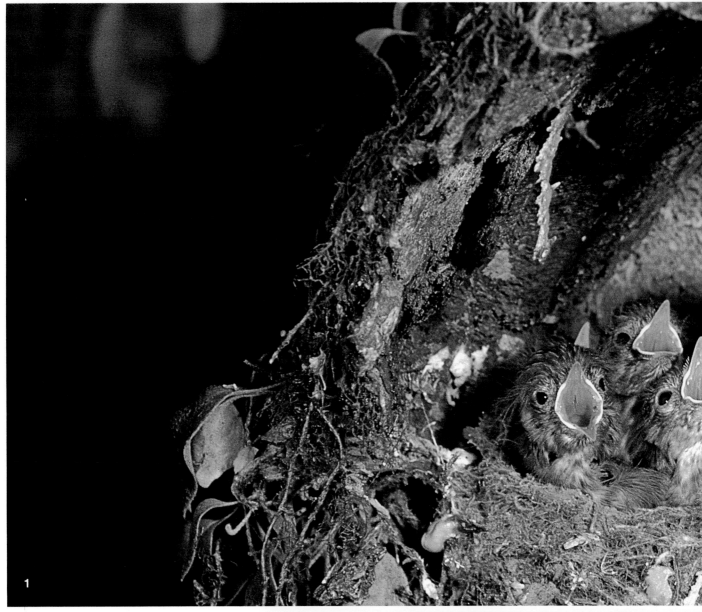

## 1 Tomtit
The Tomtit is closely related to the Scarlet
Robin of Australia. It occurs on the main
islands, the Chatham Islands, Snares and
Auckland Islands in five races. The North
Island race has a white breast, the South
Island race being normally yellow-breasted but
sometimes so pale that it looks like the North
Island bird. Although the number of eggs laid
is usually given as three to four, the male bird
in the photograph will be seen to have five
young.

## 2  Robin (*Toutouwai*)
Widely but irregularly distributed in both
native and exotic forest and familiar to all who
visit its habitat. The bird illustrated is the
South Island race, North Island birds being
sooty-black above and white below. It feeds on
insects and other small invertebrates, mainly
in leaf litter and on moss-covered logs as in the
illustration. The song is surprisingly vigorous
for such a small bird.

### 3  Snares Tomtit

Occurs only on the Snares Islands, south of
Stewart Island. In plumage it differs from
the familiar Pied and Yellow-breasted Tits
of the North and South Islands in being
completely black, but does not seem to
differ in habits. The habitat is scrub,
consisting chiefly of a species of tree daisy
(*Olearia lyalli*).

43

## 1 Fantail (*Piwakawaka*)

Plentiful thoughout the North, South and Stewart Islands and the Chatham Islands, wherever there are plenty of trees, Fantails feed on insects caught in flight and frequently perform spectacular aerobatics in pursuit of their prey. The bird illustrated belongs to the North Island subspecies, those of the South Island and the Chatham Islands having progressively more white on the tail.

## 2 Bellbird (*Korimako*)

The dark gloss on head and face shows this to be a male bird, the female being duller with a pale streak on the cheek. Found in most types of native forest and scrub, the Bellbird also occurs in some exotic forests and comes into gardens and orchards close to its normal habitat. It feeds on nectar, small fruit and insects. To hear the famous morning chorus of the Bellbird is an unforgettable experience.

## 3 Silvereye (*Tauhou*)

Seen throughout New Zealand, especially in winter when it gathers in flocks, the Silvereye was first noticed in New Zealand in the 1830s. It has since become one of our most familiar native birds. It feeds on nectar, insects, berries and fruit and readily visits feeding tables in suburban gardens (which should always be placed beyond the reach of cats). The Maori name "Tauhou" means "Little Stranger".

1

**2 Whitehead** (*Popokatea*)
Found throughout most forested areas of the
North Island south of the Firth of Thames and
on Great and Little Barrier and a few other
offshore islands. It is also one of the most
successful colonists of the exotic pine forests.
The Whitehead is similar in plumage pattern
to the Yellowhead but lacks any trace of
yellow pigment. Its food consists of insects
and small native fruit.

**Yellowhead** (*Mohua*)
Restricted to beech forests of the South Island
the Yellowhead builds the same cup-type nest
as its relatives the Whitehead and Brown
Creeper, but always in a hollow tree. The
brownish tinge on the nape of the bird
illustrated shows it to be either a female or a
juvenile, probably the former. Unlike the
Whitehead and Brown Creeper, this species
does not occur in exotic forests.

# Dwellers of the Wetlands

## D. Hadden

Uncrowded beaches, bush-clad valleys rising to snow-covered peaks and lowland forests with sparkling fern-draped streams have tremendous aesthetic appeal. But who finds pleasure when the word swamp is mentioned? For many it conjures up mud… smells… uselessness. For the urban dweller, a swamp is land that will improve his property value only when it is cleaned up. For the farmer a swamp is simply more land in production when it is drained. But to the birdwatcher, swamps and wetlands conjure up thoughts of some of our most fascinating yet most threatened bird life.

Wetland areas have declined markedly in total, despite the establishment of hydro lakes, sewage ponds and small farm dams. A wildlife survey in 1962 showed 160,000 hectares of wetlands had been lost. In 1974 the figure had climbed to 263,000 hectares. In pre-European times the present site of Christchurch was largely swamp. Marsh Crakes may well have skulked where Cathedral Square is today.

Three major wetland areas still exist although much reduced. Parts of the formerly vast Waikato swamplands which were inhabited by Spotless Crake and Fernbird are now grazed by cattle. Lake Wairarapa, also considerably less extensive than before, is currently under threat of partial reclamation. At present it still contains some 90% of New Zealand's known wetland species. In the South Island, Lake Ellesmere boasts a checklist of 149 species. And although these three major areas are widely separated and would seem at first to be independent of one another, a species such as the Shoveller is well able to exploit all three areas in a short time. Even the Spotless Crake has been known to fly considerable distances between swamps. Thus, having a series of wetland areas throughout New Zealand is essential.

When wetlands are reclaimed it is those species living exclusively in marginal areas between farmland and lake that are most vulnerable. The elusive Bittern and the secretive Crake are not even noticed as the land is broken in. More adaptable species, such as the Pied Stilt, Pukeko and Paradise Shelduck have a better chance of survival. In fact, the latter two range onto farmland and successfully raise young in areas with minimal or no wetlands nearby.

By contrast, the Brown Teal which was once widespread from Northland to Stewart Island, is today rare on the mainland. The total population is a meagre 1500 birds. Faring even worse is the Black Stilt, extremely rare but currently the object of a major effort to stabilise and, if possible, increase its shrinking numbers.

Then, too, consider our rivers. The Blue Duck, once widespread, is now confined to less modified higher reaches of mountain streams. The Wrybill breeds exclusively on the larger Canterbury and North Otago river beds. At present this endemic plover appears to be maintaining its population of just 5000 birds, but whether habitat modification, through, for example, irrigation schemes, will affect its numbers remains to be seen.

Until recently the Crested Grebe of the South Island and the New Zealand Dabchick of the North Island were our only breeding grebes, but in the last ten years both the Australian Little Grebe and the Hoary Headed Grebe have been found nesting here. In fact, during this last century, New Zealand has seen a remarkable number of Australian wetland species introduce themselves to the New Zealand avifauna. River beds in Hawke's Bay became the initial colonising areas of the Black-fronted Dotterel. Today it is spreading through both islands. Another colonist has been the Spur-winged Plover, choosing Southland to establish itself, but it too has increased and is now widespread in the North Island. Both the Welcome Swallow and White-faced Heron arrived to occupy ecological niches not filled by any New Zealand bird. The only other breeding herons are the Kotuku and the marine Reef Heron but Little Egrets and Cattle Egrets are being seen in such numbers that it is quite possible that breeding colonies will be established one day. Royal Spoonbills established a small nesting colony in the 1940s but have not had the spectacular increases of the White-faced Herons. Among the ducks, the Grass Whistling Duck, White-eyed Duck, Australian Wood Duck and the Northern Shoveler have occasionally been recorded in our wetland areas.

## 1 Waders in flight

On tidal harbours and estuaries throughout New Zealand, as the tide rises to cover the feeding grounds, the Waders gather on a raised beach of exposed shell bank. The high-tide period is spent preening and sleeping; then, as the falling tide exposes the sand on mudflats, the birds become restless until they have all moved away to recommence feeding. The photograph shows, in a coastal environment, Bar-tailed Godwits, Pied Oystercatchers and Pied Stilts, the latter two of which can also be found in wetlands.

## 2 Wrybill (*Ngutu-parore*)

The Wrybill is a confiding species both in its winter haunts in the North Island and at its breeding grounds in Canterbury and North Otago. The two eggs which blend perfectly with the shingle of the river beds would make nest location very difficult were it not that a Wrybill will often return to incubate its eggs even though an observer is only a short distance away.

### 3 Banded Dotterel (*Tuturiwhatu*)

A few of New Zealand's birds migrate annually to Australia; for example, the Gannet; but amongst the waders only the Banded Dotterel does so. After breeding, those birds nesting inland move to the coast and fly north, some remaining in New Zealand but many crossing the Tasman. The Maori name Tuturiwhatu is taken from the excited trilling of the males during courtship display.

51

## 2 Spur-winged Plover

This self-introduced Australian immigrant is one of our earliest nesters, eggs sometimes being present in July. The bird pictured is just commencing to expose its brood patch, thus allowing the bare skin of the breast to warm the eggs. The wing spurs from which its name is derived are clearly visible. With its distinctive slow flapping flight and loud rattling call, the Spur-winged Plover is becoming one of our better-known species.

## 1 Black-fronted Dotterel

This striking Australian immigrant now nests widely throughout New Zealand and continues to expand its range each year. Nests are on river beds often close to water. The camouflaged eggs are very difficult to locate among the shingle but prone to destruction as a result of flash floods. Black-fronted Dotterels are often seen right at the water's edge busily searching for the tiny aquatic creatures on which they feed.

## 2 Brown Bittern (*Matuku*)

Although seldom seen, the bittern can still be found in suitable large swamps throughout the country. The booming of the male, usually at night during spring and summer, caused the Maori to call it Matuku-Kurepo, the Matuku of the swamps. Bitterns nest from late August to January, choosing dense swamp vegetation where 3–5 eggs are laid. Incubation takes 25 days. Chicks are fed on regurgitated frogs, eels and various other swamp denizens.

## 1 Pied Stilt (*Poaka*)

Well known to birdwatchers, the Pied Stilt is now the commonest breeding wader in New Zealand, having increased its numbers by quickly adapting to the additional open land available through farming. It defends its nest site by "barking" vociferously and then attacking the intruder. Should he persist, a broken-wing display is given, accompanied by the most pleading cries imaginable.

**1**

**1 Grey Teal** (*Tete*)
The Grey Teal introduced itself to New
Zealand over a century ago and although now
widespread, is common in only a few favoured
localities. It is found on lakes, lagoons and
rivers of both islands, but possibly a lack of
suitable nesting sites (it seems to prefer holes
in trees) prevents it increasing in numbers
more rapidly. The Grey Teal is one of our
smallest ducks. It lacks head markings but has
a white triangle on the upper wing,
conspicuous in flight.

**Previous page Black Stilt** (*Kaki*)
Unlike the Pied Stilt, the Black Stilt has
declined in numbers until today its continued
survival is threatened. It may be found
nesting only within the Waitaki River System
where recently fenced areas have afforded it a
measure of protection. After nesting, some
birds disperse as far as the North Island as
black and smudgy coloured birds are seen
from time to time near Auckland.

## 2 New Zealand Shoveler
### (Kuruwhengi)
Smaller than the Mallard and Grey Duck, the male Shoveler (female is pictured) is strikingly coloured. The chestnut underparts contrast with the blue upperwing coverts and the white flank patch. A prominent white line in front of the eye stands out from the bluish-grey head. Shovelers seem to prefer rank grassy areas fairly near water to construct their down-lined nests. About 12 eggs are laid and incubation lasts 25 days.

## 3 Paradise Shelduck (Putangitangi)
This species is often seen in pairs, the white head of the female contrasting with the male's dark colours. The calls of male and female differ markedly and are well known to hunters who find the deep *zonk-zonk* of the male and the shrill *zeek-zeek* of the female less than helpful as they sound the alarm when disturbed in a mountain valley.

### 1 Blue Duck (*Whio*)

The Blue Duck is usually only met with in the more turbulent upper reaches of mountain streams, where it is easily overlooked as it stands quietly amongst the tumbled boulders. When disturbed it often slips into the rapids and disappears downstream. Nests are well concealed close to water and soon after hatching, the chicks fearlessly accompany their parents in the fast-moving waters.

### 2 Plumed Whistling Duck

More than a dozen ducks have been recorded in New Zealand but few less frequently than this rare Australian straggler known from just one sighting. It is aptly named, as not only is its call a loud piping whistle but its wings also give a distinctive whistle as it flies. A number of Australian birds have established themselves in New Zealand in the last hundred years and there is no reason to suppose this species may not at some future date be found breeding here too.

## 3 Grey Duck (*Parera*)

The Grey Duck is common and widespread throughout New Zealand although possibly declining in numbers as it competes with the introduced Mallard. Buller records that Maori in the Bay of Plenty had special duck lakes guarded by tapu until the ducks had moulted and were flightless, whereupon the whole village would join in the duck-hunting expedition. Dogs brought in ducks which were taken by the men, who bit them in the head to kill them. The ducks were then thrown behind to the women who gathered them.

3

### 1 Australian Little Grebe
The first record of this species in New Zealand was at Arrowtown in August 1968. Today it is widely distributed although not common and nesting sites are known in a number of localities. It can easily be identified in the breeding season by its patch of yellowish skin at the gape.

### 2 Royal Spoonbill
Another self-introduced Australian straggler superficially similar to herons but easily distinguished by its bill shape. When feeding, the partly open bill is moved from side to side and prey grasped in the spoon-shaped tip. A small breeding colony is known at Okarito although pairs have attempted to breed elsewhere. Nests are usually high and contain 3–4 eggs laid in November and December. During autumn and winter birds disperse to coastal regions throughout New Zealand.

### 3 New Zealand Scaup (*Papango*)
This species is New Zealand's only representative of the diving ducks. Scaups prefer clean, clear water where they dive to take food items from the lake floor. Even newly hatched chicks have been observed diving to two metres. The male is darker than the female and readily distinguished by its yellow iris, the female's being brown.

## 1 Black-billed Gull (*Tarapunga*)

Predominantly an inland gull of the South Island rivers and lakes, this species has recently expanded its range within the North Island. For many years it has nested near Rotorua but now may be found breeding near Gisborne, the Firth of Thames, and elsewhere. It differs from the Red-billed Gull not only in bill colour but in the lesser amount of black present on the first three primaries.

## 2 Black-fronted Tern (*Tara*)

The Black-fronted Tern is the common tern of inland South Island. It may be found nesting in river beds east of the Alps from Marlborough to Southland. It hawks insects but also takes fish and will follow a plough, picking up overturned grubs. After breeding they disperse to the coast, some crossing Cook Strait and wintering in the North Island.

## 1 Pukeko

The Pukeko is a conspicuous and adaptable member of our bird fauna. It is known to be polygamous and nests containing two clutches of eggs are not uncommon. Buller recorded how the Maori found them excellent eating when roasted in their own fat and he himself declared that if "hung sufficiently long and properly dressed, it makes an excellent dish… hardly to be distinguished from that of the capercailzie".

## 2 Australian Coot

Between 1875 and 1953 the Australian Coot was recorded just eight times in New Zealand, all from the South Island. A probable invasion in the mid-1950s saw coots establish themselves as breeding residents. They are still uncommon but increasing as chicks are successfully raised on lakes in both the North and South Islands. Note the lobed feet on this bird as it prepares to incubate.

2

### 2 Sacred Kingfisher (*Kotare*)

Compared with Australia's ten species, and
Papua New Guinea's 24 species, New
Zealand is poorly endowed having just two
species of kingfisher. One is the widespread
and well-known Sacred Kingfisher and the
other the introduced Laughing Kookaburra
found only between Warkworth and Albany,
north of Auckland. A kingfisher's diet
includes insects, crabs, even small birds and
skinks as depicted here. They are notoriously
bad housekeepers, their nesting hole
entrances usually defaced with droppings and
often smelling unbearably.

### 1 Little Shag (*Kawaupaka*)

This species is dimorphic, occuring in a
white-throated phase and a pied phase. They
freely interbreed although the former is more
common. Buller found that Maori in earlier
days "owned" colonies of Little Shags so that
in the breeding season they could gather the
young birds and pot them, considering them a
great delicacy. The bird depicted has its head
feathers raised in a display of alarm.

## 1 White Heron (*Kotuku*)

Rare in New Zealand but widespread and common from Australia to India, the Kotuku attracts public attention wherever one is sighted during its autumn dispersal from its one breeding area near Okarito. In the North Island its rarity has passed into a Maori proverb "He kotuku rerenga tahi" indicating it would only be seen "once in a lifetime". The highly prized plumes of the White Heron along with those of the Huia were kept in carved boxes and used by chiefs.

**2  Southern Crested Grebe** (*Puteketeke*)
Nests are constructed of swamp vegetation and although usually surrounded by water, are often given stability by being anchored to a submerged branch. Crested Grebes feed primarily on fish (55%), along with insects (32%) and plant material (13%). Food is taken underwater, dives lasting about 20–30 seconds although times of over 1 minute have been recorded.

### 1 Banded Rail (*Mohopereru*)

Like our two small Crakes, the Banded Rail is secretive in nature, usually only being glimpsed as it scurries into the mangroves bordering a tidal estuary north of Auckland. Banded Rails quickly become scarce south of Auckland and South Islanders may observe them only in northwest Nelson. Nests are usually well concealed and as can be seen here, reeds are sometimes pulled together to form an arch above the nest.

### 2 White-faced Heron

This self-introduced Australian species has become widespread throughout New Zealand. Favouring tall trees as nest sites, eggs are laid from June to December and both parents help incubate the eggs and feed the chicks. A wide variety of aquatic foods is taken, ranging from coastal mudflat items to the introduced Australian Green Frog found widely in freshwater swamps.

**1 Spotless Crake** (*Puweto*)
A shy bird, this species is seldom seen except when attracted into the open by its tape-recorded calls. The bird illustrated is slipping onto its nest constructed in a small patch of cuttygrass growing in a raupo swamp. Remarkably small swamp remnants have been found to contain breeding pairs. Incubation takes about 21 days and adults have been seen eating the eggshells of newly hatched chicks.

**2 New Zealand Dabchick** (*Weweia*)
The Maori name for this species as with the names for many other New Zealand birds is an onomatopoeic description of its call. Dabchicks are completely aquatic, building floating nests and seeking molluscs and insects among the shallow waters of North Island lakes. Like other grebes, dabchicks have lobed instead of webbed feet and also carry their young on their backs.

### Harrier (*Kahu*)

This almost ubiquitous "hawk" of New Zealand is a race of the Marsh Harrier, a species distributed across the Old World as far west as Britain. The New Zealand bird is probably a recent immigrant as it differs in no way from the Swamp Harrier of Australia except for its behaviour. Australian birds are normally seen flying low over swamp or grassland in search of such prey as frogs, lizards or small rodents. New Zealand does not have this variety of small animal life and the Harrier here has taken over the scavenging functions of such birds as kites, and tends to soar at high altitudes.

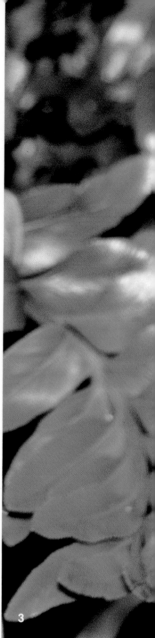

## 1 South Island Pied Oystercatcher (*Torea*)

Nesting sites include fields, river beds, lake shores and even sub-alpine tundra above the tree line. Usually two eggs are laid with incubation lasting nearly four weeks. Although this species nests only in the South Island, on the conclusion of breeding, thousands migrate to suitable North Island harbours and estuaries. Careful annual counts reveal numbers have increased markedly since 1940.

## 2 Pipit (*Pihoihoi*)

Rough open country on both mountain and coast is the preferred habitat of our native pipit. The introduced skylark favouring well-farmed pastureland is often confused with the Pipit but the Skylark has a short crest and its aerial song is unmistakable. Pipits feed largely on insects although some seeds are also eaten. While on the ground, Pipits characteristically move their tails up and down.

## 3 Snares Fernbird (*Matata*)

Five living subspecies of Fernbird are recognised, that of the Chathams now being extinct. The Snares Fernbird illustrated here is more readily seen in the open, whereas the other subspecies all keep well concealed in low fern and scrub. Its nests are hidden in thick vegetation and placed close to the ground, Stead observing that both adults incubate and that pairs are sometimes double-brooded.

# The Oceanic Birds

## J. Warham

Oceanic birds are those that range widely over the seas and resort to New Zealand only for nesting. As a distinguished seabird scientist once put it, "Seabirds can feed where they will but must nest where they can." Hence our New Zealand archipelago has long been a haven for many wide-ranging oceanic birds and it still is. They are mainly found on offshore islands free from cats, stoats and dogs. Most of the old nesting sites on the North, South and Stewart Islands have been abandoned, for the birds, having evolved in isolation from land mammals, are unable to adapt to their attacks. But there are still many millions of seabirds living here which swim or fly to deep water to feed on the rich plankton, fish and squid which support them and our local fisheries.

The most specialised of these are the penguins. These are descendants of flying birds that have turned their wings into flippers to enable them to "fly" under water. Three kinds nest on the main islands: the Blue Penguin breeds here and there along the coasts of all three islands. The Yellow-eyed Penguin lays her eggs under the flax and thickets of coastal Otago and around Stewart Island, while the Fiordland Penguin breeds in caves and forests along the southwestern and southern coasts of the South Island. The latter is one of five species of crested penguin, four of which breed in our region, mainly on the sub-antarctic islands to the south.

More plentiful both in species and individual numbers are the tubenosed birds or petrels, a group that includes the albatrosses, muttonbirds, prions and storm-petrels. They make up the most important group of birds in New Zealand. Not only do they include 22% of the different kinds of birds that breed here, but their total population could well outnumber all the rest of the New Zealand birds added together.

Many petrels fly far from their nesting places to feed along the ocean "fronts" where upwellings and current mixings bring nutrients to the surface and support big plankton, fish, squid and krill populations. One of the most abundant of these birds, the Sooty Shearwater or New Zealand Muttonbird, is used as a food resource by the Maori of the South Island who harvest some of the fat chicks each year. A different and less abundant species, the Grey-faced Petrel, is also taken off the North Island.

Perhaps the best way to see our petrels is to go out with a fisherman, for many species are habitual followers of boats. Also, if conditions are right, a wide range of albatrosses, shearwaters and petrels can be seen from the Cook Strait and Foveaux Strait ferries. Quite good sightings can be obtained too from hills and headlands overlooking the sea, particularly after storms and while on-shore winds are blowing.

A few petrels still nest on the mainland but only the Royal Albatrosses of Taiaroa Head, near Dunedin, are easily seen. Here a small group breeds on grassy slopes and can be watched from a carefully sited "hide".

The other oceanic bird whose nesting is easily seen is the Australasian Gannet. At Cape Kidnappers near Napier is the world's most accessible gannetry, and thanks to protection it has expanded in recent years. While gannets travel far (and many of our birds cross the Tasman Sea to feed in Australian waters) you can often see them off our coasts too. When the fish schools are active, gannets come right into harbours and close inshore and can be seen plummeting like missiles as they dive for food.

Related to the gannets are the shags and cormorants of which we have many kinds. All have long hooked bills adapted for holding slippery fish. The shags are the more oceanic of the two groups and they generally nest on cliffs from which they sally out to deep water. They fish by swimming underwater using their large, webbed feet to propel them, often remaining submerged for 30 seconds or more, emerging to swallow their prey on the surface.

Some of our oceanic birds stay here all the year round but several petrels migrate to the North Pacific each year after breeding. The best known of these is the Sooty Shearwater which winters in sub-arctic seas. Several banded at the Snares Islands have been found in Japanese fishing nets just south of the Aleutian Islands and the birds are abundant off California's shores as the flocks move south before their return to our seas in September.

A few of our oceanic birds are true New Zealanders, found nowhere else. The Royal Albatross, Pycroft's Petrel and the Fiordland, Erect-crested and Snares Penguins are examples. Others are found widely throughout the Southern Hemisphere. Such are the Wandering Albatross, the Rockhopper Penguin and most of the smaller albatrosses or mollymawks. But there are few cosmopolitans among these seabirds, in the sense that they breed here while other populations of the same species breed in the Northern Hemisphere. The best example is the skua, which nests on our sub-Antarctic islands and also in Scotland and Iceland, and a few petrels like the Soft-plumaged Petrels that nests here and also in the central North Atlantic at places like Madeira.

**1 Erect-crested Penguin**
Nesting only at the Antipodes and Bounty
Islands, with a few pairs at Campbell Island,
stragglers reach Australia and one even got to
the Falkland Islands. Mutual preening like
this is a common activity between members of
pairs, helping to strengthen their relationship
which is maintained from year to year. These
birds are ashore in readiness for their annual
moult and their plumage is dulled with wear.

Previous page **Snares Crested Penguin**
The Snares Islands, south of Stewart Island,
are the only breeding ground for this species.
The birds nest in rather small colonies among
tussock grass or beneath scrub and trees. At
3–4 weeks of age the chicks join with others
to form a crèche. They are no longer guarded
but both parents will visit them, usually of an
evening, with food. The adults around by day
are mostly younger birds that have yet to
breed and are unrelated to the chicks nearby.

## 2 Yellow-eyed Penguin (Hoiho)

This bird is not found outside New Zealand and seems to have no close relatives among penguins elsewhere. They are not colonial birds but nest in social groups among coastal vegetation. They occur along the east coast of the South Island to Southland, Stewart Island, Campbell Island and the Auckland Islands (where this photograph was taken) but are absent from the Antipodes, Bounty and Snares Islands, perhaps because these lack the sandy beaches on which Yellow-eyed Penguins prefer to land.

## 4 Fiordland Crested Penguin

Closely related to the Snares Crested Penguin, this species differs from it in a number of characteristics, including the presence of white cheek stripes. Fiordland Penguins are winter breeders and their chicks swim away at the end of November. As with other crested penguins, the male bird, like the one seen here on its nest, has a larger bill and is more aggressive than the female.

## 3 White-flippered Penguin

This bird, shown here returning to its nest, belongs to the Canterbury race of the Little Blue Penguin which breeds widely round New Zealand coasts. The photo illustrates the agility of the smaller kinds of penguin on land. The birds are active ashore only by night and escape summer heat and predators by nesting in burrows. They have evolved a balance of adaptations fitting them for life at sea and ashore.

### 1 Snares Crested Penguin

It is the custom among crested penguins for the males to take care of the newly hatched chick until it is 3 to 4 weeks old. These males do not leave to feed, and the females when they return about once a day, feed only the chick. The signal for the male to depart comes when the now mobile chick joins with others to form a crèche as described on page 84. The chick can now be left unguarded and the male can leave to break his fast.

### 2 Australasian Gannet

This bird is shown in the "flying up" posture which signals its imminent leap forward, probably to depart. Both eyes are being brought to bear on the ground before it, so that the bird has the benefit of binocular vision needed for accurate judgement of distance. It resembles other seabirds in having a complex "language" of display.

### 3 Australasian Gannet

The Cape Kidnappers colony is only one of many places where this big bird breeds and is the only colony confined to the New Zealand mainland. The serried ranks of nests occur because, like many colonial seabirds, the pairs site their nests just beyond pecking range of their neighbours, but no further.

### 1 Sooty Shearwater
Like other burrowing petrels, they come to and from their nests only under cover of darkness. Although magnificent fliers, they have high wing loadings and take-off is facilitated if they can jump from a high rock so that their long wings can get a grip of the air before they have lost too much height.

### 2 Sooty Shearwater
This species abounds in New Zealand seas and is often seen in huge flocks feeding close in on near-surface fish which are taken in shallow dives. The migratory streams travelling south in September and north in April and May can often be seen from vantage points along our eastern coastline.

## 1 Grey Petrel

A medium-sized seabird with a circumpolar range, in New Zealand it breeds only on Antipodes Island. It is a winter nester, using underground burrows occupied by other kinds of petrel during the summer. The Grey Petrel is a magnificent flier and dives well, swimming underwater using its wings. It is also quite agile on land, as this photograph shows. Coloured leg bands make it possible to check the identity of individual birds without further handling.

## 2 Northern Giant Petrel

In the Southern Ocean these birds perform the role that vultures do in the tropics, and any carrion attracts them. At large food sources like dead whales or seals, a definite hierarchy is established where only a few birds hold feeding places at the corpse. The others sit around and watch for their opportunity. While much of their posturing is mere threat, quite severe fighting may develop with the winner taking over the loser's feeding position.

## 3 Soft-plumaged Petrel

This specimen, photographed at Antipodes Island in 1969, was the first found in New Zealand and the species has still not been found elsewhere in our region apart from one or two storm-washed birds dead on our beaches. This is a rather cosmopolitan species as Soft-plumaged Petrels nest on several southern islands to the west and also on Madeira in the mid-Atlantic.

## 1  Fluttering Shearwater

A small, black-and-white "muttonbird" that lays its egg in a burrow, it breeds on many islands in Cook Strait and off the east coast of the North Island. A close relative, Hutton's Shearwater, nests at about 1700m in the mountains behind Kaikoura, and both these birds in turn are related to the Manx Shearwater of the north Atlantic Ocean and the Irish Sea.

## 2 Fulmar Prion

These small and rather stubby-billed petrels
are found only in a few isolated breeding
places. In our region they occur on the Bounty,
Chatham and Snares Islands. Their single egg
is laid in a rock crevice, and on the isolated
stacks that they frequent and which usually
lack predatory skuas, Fulmar Prions are about
in broad daylight. This pair was courting, a
process involving much crooning and mutual
preening of heads and necks.

### 1 Black-bellied Storm Petrel

These tubenosed birds pick up plankton foods with their bills while dancing about above the surface of the sea which they fend off with their long legs. Like other petrels they have big olfactory lobes in their brains and the raised nasal tubes may be part of their equipment to help them smell out their food.

### 2 Pycroft's Petrel

One of our endemic and rarest tubenoses, found breeding only on a few islands off the east coast of the North Island, it lays a single white egg in a burrow dug in the soil. Like some Fairy Prions it probably loses some chicks and eggs to the Tuataras that share some of its breeding haunts. Pycroft's Petrel has a light, airy flight, a chattering *ti-ti-ti* call, and is active on and over land only after dark.

### 3 Buller's Shearwater

Breeding only on the Poor Knights Islands, their numbers have expanded dramatically over recent years as they have re-colonised land once used by a Maori tribe that no longer lives there. As with most petrels, courtship involves a lot of preening of the partner's head and neck accompanied by loud caterwauling cries. They burrow under stones and lay their egg well underground.

2

3

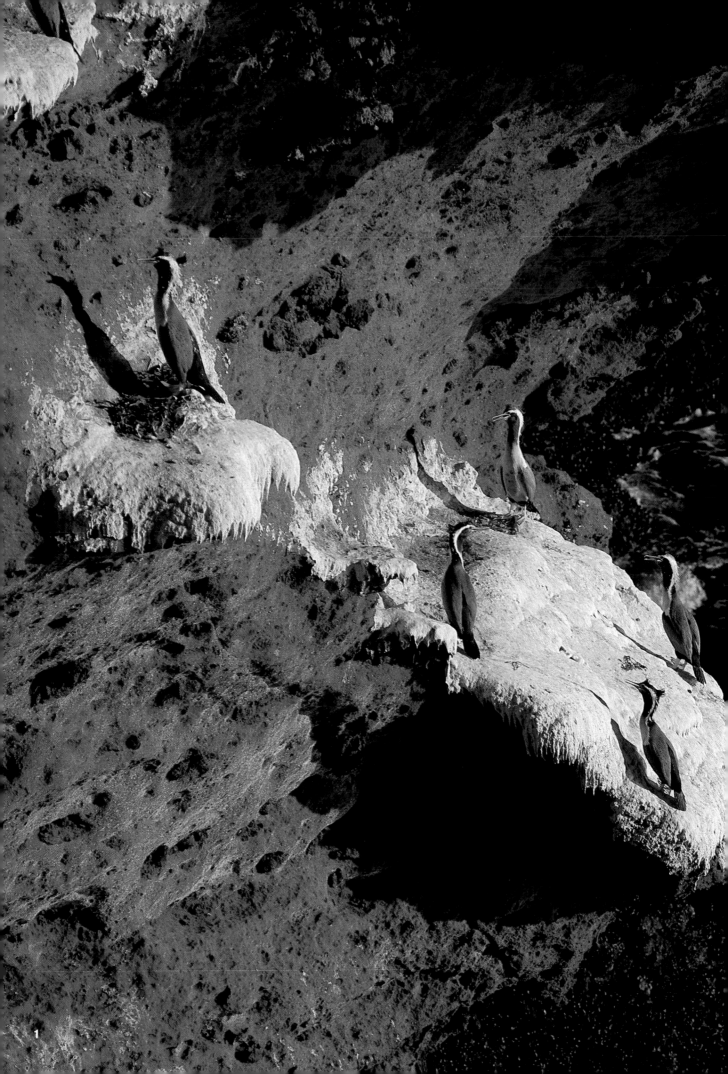

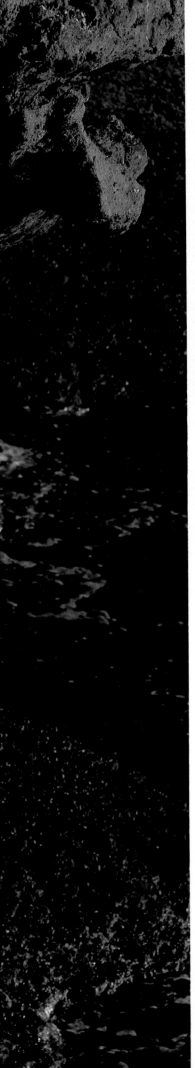

### 1 Spotted Shag
One of our few cliff-nesting birds, their colonies are to be found on ledges overlooking the sea at many points around the three main islands. They construct nests of seaweed and guano in which they raise 2 or 3 chicks. In this picture they are using narrow platforms formed where soft volcanic deposits have washed from old lava flows on Banks Peninsula.

### 2 Spotted Shag
A number of distinct "subspecies" of Spotted Shag have evolved of which this is the so-called Blue Shag, common round Stewart Island. The verdigris-green skin in front of the eyes is typical of this group of shags. The crests are worn only when the birds come into breeding condition and have almost been lost by the time the chicks hatch.

## 1 Pied Shag

Common along the coasts and in harbours and estuaries, they breed from the Three Kings Islands in the north to Stewart Island in the south. The same species is found in southern Australia. The birds may nest in trees, as here, or on cliffs. Note the greenish-blue eye rims and yellow caruncles found in both sexes.

## 2 Auckland Island Shag

This is a member of a group of New Zealand shags that shows much variation in plumage so that the birds at the three islands where they breed – Campbell, the Bounties and the Auckland Islands – are sufficiently distinct to have separate names. A related species breeds on isolated rocks in Cook and Foveaux Straits and on the Chatham Islands.

### 1 Cape Pigeon

Southern birds which breed as far south as Antarctica, they are readily identified by their checkered plumage. They commonly follow ships and sail at high speed on stiffened wings showing a magnificent control of the air. They feed on surface plankton and are common south of Cook Strait but less so north of there.

### 2 Southern Skua

These are the most widespread of our oceanic birds as they breed not only throughout the sub-antarctic zone of the Southern Ocean as their name implies, but also in the sub-arctic too. In northern Scotland they are known as Great Skuas or Bonxies. Raised wings displaying "roundels" are used in threat display.

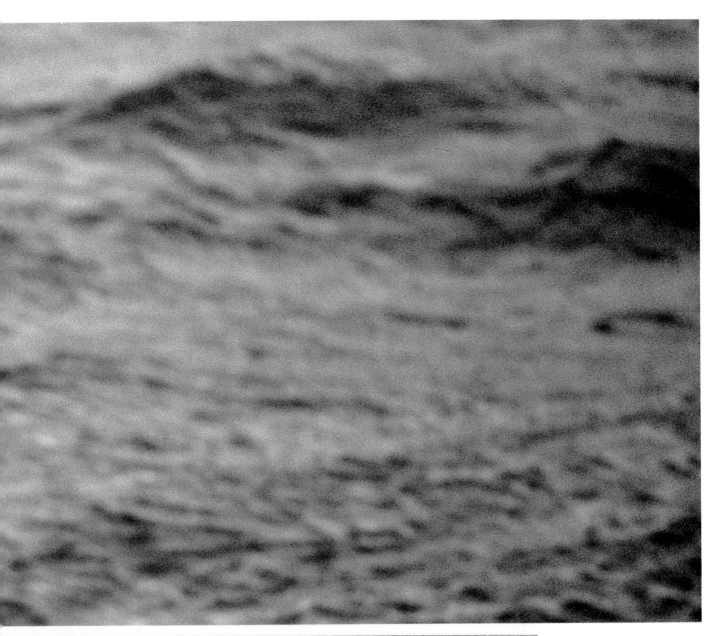

### 3 Sooty Tern

A tropical, fish-eating seabird, plentiful in the equatorial
belts of all the major oceans, it is often encountered
many days' flying from any land and is quite active after
dark. The Kermadec Island colonies, shown here, were
once large but have now almost gone due to the
depredations of cats. Like gannets, terns nest in tight
groups with just enough room between the nests to allow
movement without interfering with neighbours.

## 2 Grey-headed Mollymawk

Albatrosses and other petrels feed their chicks by regurgitating a partially digested mash of squid, crustaceans, fish and oil from their stomachs. The chick inserts its bill at an angle to that of the parent and on top of the latter's tongue so that the slurry is diverted into the chick's own gullet. They get fed perhaps every 3 or 4 days but some meals are gargantuan.

2

## Previous page 1 Southern Royal Albatross

Something like 5000 pairs of Royal Albatross nest each year at Campbell Island, but the chick grows so slowly that, as with Wandering Albatrosses, incubation and chick rearing takes about 350 days, and the birds can only breed successfully every other year. Immaturity extends over eight or nine years and it is these younger birds in particular that display in small groups like this while acquiring a mate.

## Previous page 2 Southern Royal Albatross and Cape Pigeon

Both are petrels and mixed assemblies like this one, where they have been attracted to some food resource, are often encountered. Up to seven different kinds of tubenoses may congregate around a dead whale or seal, the big albatrosses and giant petrels tearing at the flesh and the smaller birds picking up scraps and even fat droplets.

## Previous page 3 Black-browed Mollymawk

These birds breed right around the Southern Ocean, where they frequently follow ships, and also have huge colonies at Campbell Island. The Campbell Island birds are readily distinguishable from all the rest by their pale hazel-brown eyes. This bird was probably an immature in possession of a nest but without a mate.

## 1 Black-browed Mollymawk

The long, narrow wings, evolved for an energy-saving flight style called "dynamic soaring", depend on the difference between the low speed of the wind at the sea's surface and the much higher speeds well above it. The birds climb into the wind, gaining height, and when almost stopped, turn through 180° and perform a fast leeward dive. Then, as they nearly touch the sea, and flying at high speed, they turn again to make forward progression in the stiller air before climbing once more. In this way they can travel at an angle to the wind with hardly a wing beat.

## 1 Salvin's Mollymawk

This bird was named after Osbert Salvin, one-time curator of birds at the British Museum. It breeds at the Snares and Bounty Islands and is quite common in our seas, particularly around Stewart Island. It is the largest of the medium-sized albatrosses called "mollymawks" by sealers and whalers.

### 3 Light-mantled Sooty Albatross
This bird from sub-antarctic islands is seldom seen in the warmer water of "mainland" New Zealand. The courtship ritual is much simpler than that of other albatrosses, consisting of high-speed dual flights where each bird mirrors the twists and turns of its partner. On land they swing their heads skywards while sounding a loud *pee-ooo* cry, as shown here.

### 2 Black-browed Mollymawk
Mollymawks are colonial nesters and these serried rows of their mounds, in each of which a single chick is reared, are characteristic of their breeding style. This corner of one of the big Campbell Island colonies is shown at the height of the summer breeding season. The chicks are fed on fish, squid and crustaceans but, probably because the parents must travel far to feed, the meals, though large, are often irregular and the nestlings may have to fast for several days between feasts.

## 2 Buller's Mollymawk

Like other albatrosses, they have long narrow wings evolved for gliding and sailing the mainly westerly winds. Much lift is generated by these wings as they form highly efficient aerofoils. Providing that some wind is blowing, the bird has only to unfold its pinions to be airborne. Big webbed feet help to act as brakes when landing.

## 1 Buller's Mollymawk

These birds lay a single egg which is incubated by both parents in long stints, the male taking the first term of duty. This egg is cradled in a sort of egg cup made of peaty soil which hardens to provide a stable platform within which to rear the chick. This site was close to the cliff edge so the parents could sail away merely by opening their long wings as they fell into space.

# Index

**Photographic credits**

Drew K. 42 (bottom)
Fennell J. 10–11, 85 (bottom), 102 (bottom)
Hadden D. 13, 15, 17 (top), 19, 28–9, 44, 50 (bottom), 51 (bottom), 52, 61 (right), 64, 74, 75, 76 (bottom), 77 (bottom), 78, 96, 100–101
Harcourt B. 22 (top), 40, 45 (bottom), 54, 73, 97
Henderson R. 60
Jacobs W. 8, 24, 48, 66, 70, 86 (right), 87, 109
Moon G.J.H. 2–3, 6, 14, 16, 17 (bottom), 34, 36 (top), 38, 50–1 (top), 69, 72
Morris Rod front cover
National Publicity Studios 22 (bottom)
Sagar J.L. 86 (left), back cover
Sagar P.M. 27 (bottom), 31, 92, 93, 95 (top), 100 (bottom), 106 (top)
Shailer, L.C. 62 (bottom)
Smith R. 20, 23, 25, 39, 59 (bottom), 80
Soper M.F. 4, 10 (bottom), 12, 18, 27 (top), 30, 32, 35, 37, 41, 42–3, 45 (top), 46, 53, 55, 56–7, 58, 59 (top), 61 (left), 62 (top), 63, 65, 67, 68, 71, 76–7 (top), 85 (top left), 89 (bottom), 99, 101 (bottom), 102 (top), 103, 105, 107
Warham J. 26, 53 (bottom), 79, 82–3, 84, 85 (right), 88-9 (top), 90, 91, 94, 95 (bottom), 104, 106
Wildlife Service 33, 47


**Acknowledgements**

The following people provided valuable assistance:
C.N. Challies, Forest Research
Dr C.J. Burrows, Canterbury University
G. Tunnicliffe, Canterbury Museum
Sally Jacobs and Robyn Thomas

**Don Brathwaite** died in 1996 after devoting more than 30 years to the study of birds. His greatest contribution was his research into the extinct New Zealand eagle, *Harpagornis*. His knowledge of aeronautics, avian physiology and his remarkable artistic flair led to a sculpture which was adopted by the Royal New Zealand Air Force as its official emblem. He was a Member of the Royal Australasian Ornithologists' Union and the Bird Observers' Club. Don made several trips to Australia to compare the bird faunas and was the first person to record the Black-fronted Dotterel and Little Egret in New Zealand. Prior to retirement, he was an associate in ornithology at Canterbury Museum where he specialised in migrants, new colonists and extinct birds.

**Don Hadden,** who has a keen interest in bird observation and photography, is a senior teacher at Middleton Grange School. He spent seven eventful years in Papua-New Guinea during which time he discovered an unknown species of thicket warbler which was named *Cichlornis llanae* after his wife, Llane. He is the author of *99 New Zealand Birds* and *Birds of the North Solomons*. More recently he was the author and photographer of the best-selling CD-ROM *Wild South Birds of New Zealand*. Don is a Fellow of the Photographic Society of New Zealand and has gained awards in national and international photographic salons.

**John Warham** was, until his retirement in 1985, a Reader in Zoology at the University of Canterbury with research interests centred on seabirds. His doctoral study concerned the biology of crested penguins, but nowadays he works mainly on the tubenosed birds – albatrosses, shearwaters and their kin – in search of which he has travelled worldwide. He has contributed over 100 papers on their biology, as well as having organised and led several expeditions to New Zealand's sub-antarctic islands. In retirement he has published two major works on the biology of petrels and has placed an extensive bibliography of these birds on the Internet at http://www.zool.canterbury.ac.nz/jwbibpl.htm. An experienced photographer, he was elected a Fellow of the Royal Photographic Society in 1957.